*Four examples from a series of Folio Society bookmarkers, these featuring initials from the Chiswick Press in the mid nineteenth century; by Heinrich Vogeler shortly before the First World War; by Edward Wadsworth for his book 'The Black Country' of 1920; and wood engravings commissioned by the society from Elisa Trimby.*

# BOOKMARKERS

A. W. Coysh and R. K. Henrywood

Shire Publications Ltd

# CONTENTS

*Published in 1994 by Shire Publications Ltd,
Cromwell House, Church Street, Princes Ris-
borough, Buckinghamshire HP27 9AA, UK.
Copyright © 1994 by A. W. Coysh and R. K.
Henrywood. First edition 1994. Shire Album
305. ISBN 0 7478 0254 8.*

Printed in Great Britain by CIT Printing Services, Press Buildings, Merlins Bridge,
Haverfordwest, Dyfed SA61 1XF.

British Library Cataloguing in Publication Data:
Coysh, A. W. Bookmarkers. – (Shire Albums;
No. 305) I. Title II. Henrywood, R. K. III.
Series 745.9. ISBN 0-7478-0254-8.

## ACKNOWLEDGEMENTS

We would like to extend our thanks to
Jerome Betts, Helen Vellacott and the Folio Society. We are also indebted to Messrs
Dreweatt-Neate, Auctioneers, of Newbury
for the illustration of silver paper-knife
bookmarkers (page 29). All other markers shown are in the authors' collections.

Cover: *(Top) A pierced card marker embroidered with an appropriate slogan. (Left to right)
A silk marker woven by BNH Ltd of Leek for
the coronation of Edward VIII; a plastic marker
advertising Adams's Polish; and three paper
markers advertising Kolynos Dental Cream, the
Equitable Fire and Accident Office, and Pears'
Soap. (Bottom) A clip-over marker in bone or
ivory, and a wooden paper-knife marker in
Mauchline ware with a black-printed view
'Bridge from South Lowestoft'.*

*Two typical perforated card bookmarkers.
(Right) A ready-made panel with a decorated
border embroidered with a religious text and
related symbol, and mounted on a silk ribbon.
(Below) An embossed card depicting the royal
barge 'Windsor' embroidered in the reserved
panel.*

Left to right:
*A perforated card book-marker, the embroidered text embellished with a coloured print mounted on a silk ribbon.*

*A very simple home-made marker using a small chromo-lithographed Victorian Christmas card stitched to a length of coloured ribbon.*

*A Victorian ribbon marker made with a small religious watercolour sketch attached to card and sewn on to the ribbon.*

# INTRODUCTION

Few books are read at a single sitting and even when using a reference book it is often necessary to refer back to earlier pages. Something is needed to mark the place. To turn the open book upside down strains the spine; to fold down the corner of a page leaves a crease. Those who care for books use a marker. All kinds of markers are found in old books – tram tickets, postcards, slips of paper, even hairpins. However, markers prepared for the specific purpose have been used in various forms for over four hundred years. Christopher Barker, who produced the first English Bible in 1576, presented a fringed bookmarker to Queen Elizabeth I in 1584 and similar examples were soon made for church bibles, many of them still in use.

In the eighteenth century a thin silk ribbon, which could be used to keep the place, was sometimes attached to the spine. This had the advantage of always being available. Separate bookmarkers were not in common use until early Victorian times. Mary Russell Mitford in her *Recollections of a Literary Life* (1852) wrote: 'I had no marker and the richly bound volume closed instinctively.'

The earliest markers were home-made, often in the form of embroidered cards attached to ribbons, but the widespread use of the Jacquard loom in Coventry resulted in a flood of woven silk markers. In 1851 a 'Coventry ribbon' was produced for the Great Exhibition and thereafter bookmarkers were soon woven for general use.

Bookmarkers of card or stiff paper appeared in the 1880s and have provided a medium for advertising ever since. They make a fascinating study, reflecting changes in fashion and demand over the years. Although fewer in number, other markers can be found in many different materials, including leather, wood, silver, brass and early forms of plastic.

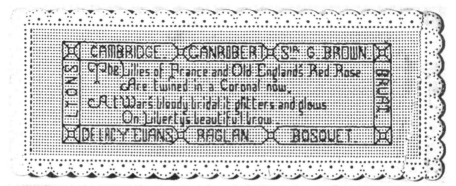

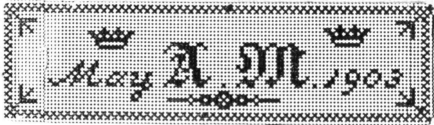

*Two dated perforated card bookmarkers, the top one embroidered with a verse and the names of the allied commanders in the Crimean War of 1853-6, the other a rather late example embroidered in 1903.*

# EMBROIDERED MARKERS

Victorian ladies taught their daughters embroidery and most young girls were expected to produce a sampler on canvas to show their skill with the needle. To embroider a small bookmarker would have been a relatively simple task. However, most embroidered markers employ small sheets of perforated card instead of canvas. Suitable card was available from stationers of the day, either in plain sheets suitable for cutting to size or ready-made with a decorated border. A few examples have been noted with the perforated panel as part of an embossed design, one attractive example featuring the royal barge *Windsor*. Any chosen design could then be sewn through the perforations, usually with cross stitch or chain stitch. Most examples are embroidered with silk, cotton or wool, and the completed card was usually sewn on to a wide ribbon for use in the book. Children typically chose simple designs – a cross, a name or a short text. Bookmarkers of this type were sometimes sent instead of a birthday card.

Adults embroidered more intricate designs to mark special occasions. Several have been noted dating from the Crimean War of 1853-6, one bearing this brief verse:

> The Lilies of France and Old England's
>   Red Rose
> Are twined in a Coronal now
> At War's bloody bridal it glitters and
>   glows
> On Liberty's beautiful brow

Around the edges are the names of the allied commanders: Bosquet, Brown, Bruat, Cambridge, Canrobert, de Lacy Evans, Lyons and Raglan.

Embroidered markers can be found with many other subjects but by the end of the nineteenth century they had been largely superseded by other types, particularly of woven silk or paper. The latest embroidered marker noted by the authors is dated 1903. In more recent times there has been a revival in needlework, particularly in tapestry, and some simple markers can be found in cross stitch on canvas.

4

# WOVEN SILK MARKERS

By the 1860s attractive machine-woven markers were being manufactured, mainly in Coventry, the centre of the silk-ribbon industry. One of the earliest was produced by J. & J. Cash to mark the death of the Prince Consort in 1861. Within a short time Thomas Stevens, pre-eminent in the field, claimed to have nine hundred different designs. Silk markers were also made by the Coventry firms of J. Caldecott, Dalton & Barton, W. H. Grant and Welch & Lenton, and in Leamington Spa, Warwickshire, by Edward Bollans & Company. Some later examples bear the mark of BNH Ltd of Leek, Staffordshire. Each marker was folded at the lower end to form a point to which a small silk tassel was attached, although this is often missing from surviving examples. The name of the maker is usually to be found on the back of the folded silk.

In 1874 Welch & Lenton registered a Miners' Union bookmarker which carried the words: 'God Bless the British Miner; what would the country do without him?' Stevens's last design, marking the opening of the first Sunday school, was registered in 1880.

Some manufacturers set up their looms at trade exhibitions weaving markers on the spot for sale to visitors. Thomas Stevens installed a loom in the machinery department at the Crystal Palace Exhibition of 1868 to weave a marker showing a portrait of Sir Joseph Paxton MP, the designer of the building which had originally been erected in Hyde Park for the Great Exhibition of 1851. Stevens and other firms are known to have woven bookmarkers at the following events:

*Two commemorative silk markers: (left) woven by Thomas Stevens of Coventry at the 1868 Crystal Palace Exhibition; (right) woven by E. Bollans & Company of Leamington Spa, marking the marriage of Princess Louise to the Marquis of Lorne in 1871.*

| | |
|---|---|
| 1865 | International Exhibition, Dublin |
| 1866 | Yorkshire Fine Art and Industrial Exhibition |
| 1867 | Coventry and Midland Manufacturing, Industrial and Art Exhibition |
| 1868 | The Crystal Palace Exhibition |
| 1869 | South Staffordshire Industrial and Fine Art Exhibition, Wolverhampton |
| 1876 | The Centennial Exhibition, Philadelphia, USA |
| 1879 | The Yorkshire Fine Art and Industrial Exhibition |
| 1893 | The World's Fair, Columbia Exposition |

*Three typical woven silk markers with religious texts, all made by Thomas Stevens of Coventry in the period around 1870.*

6

Other silk markers were woven to commemorate notable marriages and deaths and other important events, including:

1854   The opening of the Crystal Palace at Sydenham, with a portrait of the architect, Sir Joseph Paxton
1861   The death of HRH Prince Albert, the Prince Consort
1862   The Handel Festival at the Crystal Palace
1863   The marriage of Albert Edward and Alexandra, the Prince and Princess of Wales, at St George's Chapel, Windsor
1865   General Grant's victories at Vicksburg and Fort Donaldson in the American Civil War
1881   The death of Benjamin Disraeli, the Earl of Beaconsfield
1887   Queen Victoria's Golden Jubilee
1901   The death of Queen Victoria
1910   The death of King Edward VII
1937   The abortive coronation of King Edward VIII

The silk markers produced for general use vary greatly in size. Large, wide examples were for family Bibles, medium-length for books in general, and small markers for prayer-books. The Bible or prayer-book markers usually bear a cross or biblical text.

In recent times J. & J. Cash of Coventry have revived the production of woven bookmarks and present them within a folded card. One of these cards states that 'two thousand two hundred and twenty Jacquard cards are needed to weave the design and each bookmark takes half-an-hour to weave'.

Silk markers should never be folded. This may well cause them to split. They are best laid on stiff card and covered with transparent plastic.

*Three woven silk markers: (left) with greetings, made by Thomas Stevens of Coventry and London; (above) by E. Bollans & Company of Leamington Spa; and (right) by Welch & Lenton of Coventry. The representation of a £5 note is most impressive.*

7

In loving remembrance of

## Eliza Emma Livesley,

Who entered into rest

April 29th, 1918,

In her 73rd Year;

Interred Stockport Borough

Cemetery, May 2nd, 1918.

□

Life's race well run,
Life's work well done,
Life's crown well won;
Now comes rest.

———

"She hath done what she could."

———

"Peace, perfect peace."

□

*63 Great Portwood Street,*
*Stockport,*

Left to right: *A fine woven silk marker registered by Thomas Stevens of Coventry in May 1871; the detailed design features Eliza Cook's poem 'The Old Arm Chair' together with a music score for the first verse. A typical religious woven silk marker with a text on a black background, this one made by Welch & Lenton of Coventry. A printed silk marker, unusually commemorating the funeral at Stockport of a lady who died towards the end of the First World War.*

8

*Three advertisement markers featuring soap. The example on the left portraying the London skyline is one of a monochrome series issued by the London agency Day & Son of Berners Street, mostly advertising a range of household necessities. The other two, for Wright's Coal Tar Soap and Dr Lovelace's Soap, are both attractively printed in colour.*

# MARKERS OF STIFF PAPER OR CARD

By the 1880s the production of woven silk markers was declining and printed markers made of stiff paper or card began to appear in significant numbers. This development paralleled the wider availability of books themselves, and the range of available bookmarkers soon expanded dramatically. The vast majority of markers found by collectors are of paper or card, and their subject matter provides a useful means of subdivision.

## ADVERTISEMENT MARKERS

As the production of woven silk markers declined, the possibility of using cheap printed markers for advertisement purposes did not go unheeded and markers were soon promoting all sorts of house-hold necessities. Some of the earliest were produced by a London agency, Day & Son of Berners Street, which used a silhouette of the London skyline as its trademark. Each bookmark issued by this firm carried six to eight advertisements, mainly for household goods such as matches, infant foods, soap and wallpaper. Advertisements for soap predominated since it was an essential commodity demanded by a cult of cleanliness amongst the middle classes, and many firms produced their own markers. These included the East Lancashire Soap Company, the Liverpool Patent Soap Company, Dr Lovelace's Soap, Sunlight Soap and Wright's Coal Tar Soap. Some particularly attractive shaped markers were issued by Pears'

9

Soap in the 1890s.

Perfume, chocolate and sewing machines were all advertised on markers, as were some large commercial stores. Writing materials formed another category, and examples noted include Quink and Swan inks, St James's Vellum writing paper and even a Typhoo Tea 'new vacuum fountain pen'.

Many markers were produced in colour and a few were made in unusual shapes.

One in the shape of a toothpaste tube advertised Kolynos Dental Cream. Another, based on a circular plate, was patented by 'Green's Agency' to advertise Booths' Silicon China, a six-person dinner service for £6.

Markers were produced in large numbers by insurance companies. In the first decade of the twentieth century they were seriously concerned about the impending National Insurance Act which was intro-

*Three more attractive colour-printed markers advertising Owbridge's Lung Tonic, Brown & Polson's cornflour and Cadbury's chocolate and cocoa. The last of these is one of a series depicting English industries, this one featuring Northamptonshire boots.*

Left: *Two shaped bookmarkers advertising Booths' Silicon China and Pears' Soap. The pierced eyelets and strings suggest that these were originally attached to the spines of books.*

Two small paper markers issued by the Eagle Star & British Dominions Insurance Company to advertise its 'All-in Policy' for householders and house-owners. The later coloured version depicts a fire caused by a cigarette.

duced by Lloyd George and finally passed in 1911. The result was a flood of advertising and promotional bookmarkers providing a fascinating and specialised field for collectors. Companies include:

The British Dominions General Insurance Company Ltd
Eagle Star & British Dominions Insurance Company Ltd
The Edinburgh Life Assurance Company
The Equitable Fire Insurance Office
The Friends Provident Institution
Guardian Assurance Company Ltd
Law, Union & Rock Insurance Company Ltd
The Liverpool & London & Globe Insurance Company
The London & Lancashire Insurance Company Ltd
North British & Mercantile Insurance Company
Northern Assurance Company Ltd
The Prudential Assurance Company Ltd
Rock Life Assurance Company
Royal Exchange Assurance
The Scottish Widows Fund (Mutual) Life Assurance Society

Several of these insurance company markers include pictorial material of special interest. The Northern Assurance Company produced several different markers on green or cream card with

views. These include a yachting scene and views of Aldeburgh in Suffolk, Holyrood Palace, the Forth Bridge, Waterloo Bridge, the Houses of Parliament and St Paul's Cathedral.

The Prudential Assurance Company, claiming to be 'the largest insurance institution in the British Empire', issued markers with a tear-off portion which potential insurers could return by post, asking for details. One describes their 'Heritage' policy, another a 'Guaranteed Income' policy for retirement. The reverse was usually headed 'Notes of books to read' with room for ten or more titles.

The Royal Exchange Assurance Company, the oldest insurance firm in Britain, issued several different markers. One shows the earlier buildings, both destroyed by fire in 1666 and 1838 respectively, with a view of the Victorian building of 1844. Another carries the figure of a Royal Exchange fireman of 1832.

11

Five monochrome markers issued by the Northern Assurance Company of London and Aberdeen. The three on the left show the Houses of Parliament (dated 1913), St Paul's Cathedral (1905) and Aldeburgh in Suffolk (1903), the dates appearing alongside the accumulated funds for the year on the reverse. The fourth has an earlier yachting scene and the fifth has been turned to show a typical back.

Three monochrome markers issued by the Royal Exchange Assurance Corporation, one showing a fireman of 1832 and another the three Royal Exchange buildings in London dating from 1569, 1669 and 1844. In each case the reverse lists the company's various branch and district offices.

The Scottish Widows Fund issued several series of markers which are now keenly sought by collectors. The earliest were illustrated with black and white reproductions of pictures – a country scene with a prominent tree, a castle beside a lake, and 'The Wreath of May Blossom' showing children picking flowers, all unattributed. Others can be attributed to particular artists, including Artz, Ambrogis, Boronomi, Dumont and Gainsborough. Later issues were in colour and bear the title and the name of the artist. These include:
'A Shop in Venice', after Boronomi
'The Pool of London', by Vicat Cole
'The Waefu' Heart', after Thomas Duncan
'Dolly Varden', by W. S. Frith
'The Village Bridegroom', after Greuze

'Katie's Letter', after Haynes King
'Equestrian Portrait', by Landseer and Millais
'St Paul's', after David Law
'Uncle Toby and the Widow Woman', by C. R. Leslie
'June in the Austrian Tyrol', by John Macwhirter
'Off Valparaiso', by T. Somerscales
'A Hostage', after Alvarez Dumont

*Three typical Scottish Widows Fund markers printed with reproductions of paintings: an untitled country scene, 'The Wreath of May Blossom', and 'A Hostage' after E. Alvarez Dumont. These examples are monochrome but the third and some others were also printed in colour. The reverse features a medallion almost certainly designed for the society by Walter Crane.*

*Three more Scottish Widows bookmarkers, these with panels representing January, April and November from a set of twelve, all designed by Walter Crane.*

The most interesting of the company's markers are those designed by the famous artist Walter Crane (1845-1915). There are twelve designs, one for each month of the year. At the time of the first issue the company issued a free set to anyone who cared to apply. These Walter Crane illustrations have now been reproduced, by permission, on a series of markers advertising Old Grindles Bookshop in Edinburgh.

POSTCARD BOOKMARKERS
Among the early markers were bookmarks in the form of postcards measuring only 5¹/₂ inches (140 mm) in length and 1³/₄ inches (44 mm) in width. They could

be sent through the post under certain conditions. As they were treated as printed matter the only writing allowed was a signature on the picture side and a small space on the stamp side for the name and address of the sender. Many examples seem to have been posted in the 1903-4 period.

These markers were mainly made by three firms: Beagles, Rotary and Raphael Tuck & Sons. A few featured views, usually seascapes, and there were some animal pictures, but the majority were full-length portraits, sometimes of royalty, musicians or soldiers, but overwhelmingly of actors and actresses. Typical examples include Dorothea Baird, Mrs Benson,

14

Esmé Beringer, Clara Butt, Miriam Clements, Constance Collier, Madge Crichton, Marie Dainton, Lily Hanbury, Annie Hughes, Henry Irving, Lillah McCarthy, Olive May, Olive Morrell, Edmund Payne, Louie Pounds, Forbes Robertson, Marie Studholme and Irene Vanburgh.

*Four typical postcard bookmarkers: one with kittens punningly titled 'Playful Mowers', published by Rotary; one depicting Sir Henry Irving, also by Rotary; another showing Madge Crichton, published by J. Beagles & Company; and the fourth with a painting of St Anthony's Lighthouse at Falmouth, Cornwall, produced by Raphael Tuck & Sons. The last two were both postally used in 1904.*

15

## BOOKMARK CALENDARS

A number of bookmarkers were issued to serve a double purpose, an advertisement on one side and a calendar on the reverse. One of the earliest was issued by the biscuit manufacturers Peak Frean & Company in 1879. This has a group of coloured figures on the advertising side and features the prevailing postal rates on the calendar side. A Brown & Polson marker for 1884 titled a 'Portrait Bookmark' carries a portrait of the Victorian novelist W. M. Thackeray. The Equitable Fire and Accident Office used both sides for their calendars, six months on each, with examples noted dating between 1894 and 1898.

Bookmark calendars were also issued as greetings cards. One series of these includes views of places such as Brougham

Castle in Westmorland (now Cumbria) and Walberswick in east Suffolk. The earliest seems to date from 1909, the latest from 1927, which states in small print 'Mildmay No. 1477'. They were issued for Christmas, the New Year, or simply as 'Greetings from …', leaving a space for the donor's name. One anonymous calendar bookmark dating from 1937 is folded like a narrow greetings card but has only a rural scene on the outside with no space for any inscription.

Although, as with other markers, these are predominantly made of printed card, a few woven calendar bookmarkers have appeared in more recent times. One good example was issued in 1975 by Mellor Brothers of Macclesfield, a specialist manufacturer of woven labels and Jacquard trimmings.

*Opposite: Three greetings-type calendar bookmarkers, two with the calendar for 1909 on the reverse, the third dating from 1927. All three are inscribed 'Mildmay', presumably the manufacturer, and feature religious quotations on the back. The top two depict Walberswick and Brougham Castle.*

Left: *Three attractive colour-printed calendar bookmarkers issued by Peak Frean & Company (calendar for 1879 on the reverse), the Equitable Fire and Accident Office Ltd (1898) and Brown & Polson's (1884). The third is one of a series of portrait bookmarks, this one depicting W. M. Thackeray (1811-63).*

## TRANSPORT BOOKMARKERS

Bookmark advertising was used by carriers and railway companies, mainly in the period from 1900 to 1939. Pickfords issued one card with three views showing the changes from horse-drawn transport to motor lorries for household removals.

Railway bookmarkers include one attractive series which the Great Western Railway used in their books of *Holiday Haunts*. Each marker has an oval black and white view of one of the attractive areas served by the company, and on the reverse a description of the locality illustrated. These include St Michael's Mount, Tintern Abbey, the Vale of Llangollen, Gloucester Cathedral and Warwick Castle. The London & North Eastern Railway issued markers with views of the Lake District, and some simple markers were used by the London Midland & Scottish

Railway to promote holidays in Ireland and their 'Save to Travel' scheme.

Shipping lines also used bookmarker advertising. One White Star Line bookmarker was issued by Harrods Ltd and a Union Castle Line marker carries an advertisement for the Standard Bank of South Africa on the reverse. Other lines to issue attractive and colourful markers include the Royal Mail Line, the Pacific Line and the Blue Funnel Line of Alfred Holt & Company.

In 1974 Elgin Court Designs issued several markers, one with an attractive scene by Cecil Aldin called 'The Stage Coach', and other modern markers feature famous locomotives such as *Mallard* or *Flying Scotsman*. Many of these commercial markers are intended for use as gift tags with 'To' and 'From' sections printed on the reverse.

*Transport-related markers: one printed in colour for the famous Pickfords removal firm, the reverse advertising their travel agency; two from a famous set of 'Holiday Haunts' issued by the Great Western Railway, these showing Warwick Castle and the Vale of Llangollen; and one advertising the Union Castle Line.*

## BOOK-TRADE MARKERS

Bookmarkers provide an obvious advertising medium for both publishers and booksellers. Publishers often use markers to advertise a particular book or a series of volumes. Dent & Sons used them to draw notice to their Everyman Library, both for the series and for individual books. Some carried a portrait of a noted author with a quotation from his works – Milton and Sir Philip Sidney are commonly found. A red marker was issued in 1949 to announce the publication of the *New Everyman Encyclopaedia*. T. Nelson & Company issued a marker listing their sixpenny classics. Other publishers who used markers include A. & C. Black, W. & R. Chambers, Webb & Bower and Michael Joseph.

Markers have often been used to publicise a single book, sometimes in the form of an order form for the use of booksellers. Most bookmarkers of this type issued by publishers can be dated by studying publication details listed in dictionaries of literary biographies. For example, one undated bookmarker by Thomas Nelson & Sons announcing the publication of Conan Doyle's *Micah Clarke* can be dated to 1899.

Some booksellers issued their own bookmarkers, among them B. H. Blackwell of Oxford, who commissioned E. N. New, who worked with C. R. Ashbee at the Essex House Press, to design a bookmarker showing a view of the bookshop in Oxford and the proposed site of the new Bodleian Library. It was replaced with a marker showing the finished building. D. M. Beach of High Street, Salisbury, issued a design by Eustace Nash. Other booksellers who issued their own markers include George's of Bristol, Heffer's of Cambridge and Old Grindles Bookshop in Edinburgh. Many modern chains issue promotional markers, amongst them Dillons, Waterstones and Websters.

Four typical paper markers issued by J. M. Dent & Sons to promote either 'Everyman's Library' or 'Everyman's Encyclopaedia'. The example depicting Sir Philip Sidney is one of a series, others featuring Milton, Shelley and Carlyle.

A selection of book-trade markers; one for the Nelson Library of sixpenny classics (costing 7d each!); another for the joint Oxford and Cambridge 'New English Bible'; a third promoting the Whitbread Book of the Year prize for 1985; and a fourth advertising book tokens.

*Three typical modern markers: the first advertising Oliver Goldsmith's 'History of the Natural World', issued by Hammick's Bookstore; the second featuring Catherine Cookson's 'The Parson's Daughter' along with a Cookson exhibition and (on the reverse) a play based on her novel 'The Fifteen Streets', touring in 1988; the third promoting a 'green book fortnight' sponsored by 'The Observer'.*

*Four bookmarkers issued by famous bookshops: Blackwell's of Oxford, Heffer's of Cambridge, George's of Bristol, and Old Grindles Bookshop of Edinburgh.*

The Booksellers' Association has also issued markers listing the nominations for the 'Whitbread Book of the Year' and similar markers for the Booker Prize have been issued since at least 1982, including one for the prize's 25th anniversary in 1993.

In the 1970s the Folio Society issued some original bookmarkers attached to postcards encouraging members to introduce their friends to the society. They all feature the word 'Bookmark' assembled from the initial letters used in old books to start new chapters. These include decorative initials from books published in 1509, 1600, 1670 and 1889. Other examples feature initials used by the Dolphin Press in 1900, and others designed by Heinrich Vogeler in the 1900-10 period, and by N. Pusirevsky of Riga in 1924. They also used the work of artists such as Edward Wadsworth and commissioned others such as Elisa Trimby.

**OLD GRINDLES BOOKSHOP BOOKMARK**

**OLD GRINDLES BOOKSHOP**

3 SPITTAL STREET
EDINBURGH EH3 9DY
TEL: 031-229 7252

*The Observer, from a set of 12 by Walter Crane, 1913 is reproduced by kind permission of Scottish Widow's Fund and life Assurance Society, 15 Dalkeith Road, Edinburgh*

## LIBRARY BOOKMARKERS

A great many libraries print bookmarkers which are freely available to readers. Some inform readers when the libraries will be closed at holiday times and many give the opening hours. Some are printed for a particular library but many are issued by city or county libraries with many branches. The Hampshire County Library issues a long set of markers with headings such as 'Good Reads', 'Golden Oldies' and 'Modern Novels', each with a list of authors whose books fall under the relevant heading.

Many library markers inform readers of facilities of which they might otherwise be unaware, informing them about book reservations, regular book lists or facilities for obtaining specialist books for students or researchers. One library bookmarker lists 78 books by Agatha Christie with the heading 'Have You Read Them All?'.

*Two markers from a series sponsored by the Trustee Savings Bank for its local public library at Andover, Hampshire. Each has an advertisement on one side and details about the library on the reverse.*

Occasionally one may come across a marker which was issued by firms such as Boots, Mudie's, W. H. Smith or Timothy White's, all of which ran subscription libraries in their stores. Mudie's Library was established as early as 1842. Boots and W. H. Smith combined their subscription tokens with bookmarkers which could be attached to the borrowed book by using a metal clip or a cord threaded through a metal loop fixed to the spine of the book.

*Three typical library bookmarkers. Two promote local attractions, the theme park at Thorpe Park near Chertsey, Surrey, and 'The Oxford Story', an exhibition history of the famous university. The third is a commemorative marker, also from Oxford.*

21

## WARTIME BOOKMARKERS

During the Second World War of 1939-45 the use of paper was restricted and only bookmarkers related to the war effort were issued. Several include patriotic messages such as 'Save paper and sink Hitler'. Among other official examples were those showing the Spitfire and Hurricane fighter planes and a battleship – HMS *Nelson*.

There were, however, several markers appealing to the public for support. One asking for contributions to build huts for canteens, clubs and hostels was issued by the Young Women's Christian Association. Another asked for contributions towards the Overseas League Tobacco Fund, an appeal backed by General Montgomery. A third appealing for books for sailors was issued by the Royal Naval War Libraries. Markers of this type often note that the organisation concerned was registered under the War Charities Act of 1940.

*Four markers dating from the Second World War. The first two appeal for donations for the Overseas League Tobacco Fund and the YWCA Hut Fund; the others are from a series of patriotic markers, these showing the Spitfire and Hurricane and the battleship HMS Nelson.*

## APPEALS, INFORMATION AND PROPAGANDA

Bookmarkers have been commonly used to advertise charitable appeals and to disseminate information. When a National War Bonds campaign was launched in 1917 offering savings certificates, a marker offered them at 15s 9d with an assurance that at the end of five years they could be 'cashed for a sovereign'. Surprisingly, these markers carried a swastika, then a sign of good luck but later to become the official symbol of the Nazis.

In the postwar period it was common practice for public bodies to issue book-markers, good examples being the Central Council for Health Education, the Health and Cleanliness Council and the Royal Society for the Prevention of Accidents. The latter organisation issued a long series covering topics such as dangerous litter, fireworks, road safety and accidents in the home. Many charitable organisations including the Samaritans, the British Kidney Patient Association and the Children's Society print bookmarkers to inform people of their work, and local authorities use them to inform people of their services.

Every day 8 people are killed or injured in road accidents involving dogs—and hundreds of dogs are killed. Simple, sensible training will stop this happening to your pet!

ELIZABETH WARD

Having been the mother of a beloved only son, who joined the large family of kidney patients at the age of 13 and died 21 years later after 12 years on dialysis and three kidney transplants, I know only too well the trauma, heartache and despair suffered by so many kidney patients and those that love them.

Since founding the Association in 1975, I have been able to significantly improve the lot of the many hundreds of kidney patients in this country who are unable to help themselves. I have been able to provide life-saving dialysis facilities for children, fund the salaries of consultants, renal social workers and dieticians when the funds were not forthcoming from the Department of Health and in many cases award welfare grants.

But no matter how much I understand or how deeply I care, nothing, absolutely nothing can be achieved without the generous support of others. So I beg of you, give me that support, and let us together make their lives worth having.

God bless —
Elizabeth Ward

**THE BRITISH KIDNEY PATIENT ASSOCIATION**
BORDON, HANTS.

**S**
suicide?
despair?
*who cares?*

**SALISBURY
(0722) 23355**
*IS MANNED—DAY AND NIGHT—8₁*

**the samaritans**

Are you ordinary enough to be one of them?

You need to be a good listener, who understands how other people feel and wants to help them as a friend.

We will give you a series of preparatory talks to help you with the work.

If you feel you might not be able to cope but would like to try, you are probably the type we are looking for.

The Samaritans, too, need friends. To support what they do you can collect or subscribe money and do other administrative duties which they have not time to carry out themselves.

Write to
**THE DIRECTOR
THE SAMARITANS of
SALISBURY & DISTRICT
42 MILFORD STREET
SALISBURY SP1 2BP**

And REMEMBER, if you are suicidal or despairing, you can talk to the Samaritans in complete confidence, any hour - day or night.

**DEAR GOD**

Thank you for loving me and for giving me my family and friends.

Please help THE CHILDREN'S SOCIETY to care for other children and help me to care about them too.

Give me a joyful heart and helping hands, so that your love can be seen in all I do.

I ask this in Jesus' name.

AMEN

*One of a series of markers issued by the Royal Society for the Prevention of Accidents, and three typical charity bookmarkers, these from the British Kidney Patient Association, the Salisbury branch of the Samaritans and the Children's Society.*

## COMMEMORATIVE MARKERS

Many of the woven silk markers issued in Victorian times were commemorative and, although they are less commonly found, markers have been issued ever since to mark special occasions. Examples inevitably include royal events, including Queen Victoria's Diamond Jubilee of 1897, her death in 1901, the death of King Edward VII in 1910, Queen Elizabeth II's Silver Jubilee in 1977, and several markers inspired by the marriage of the Prince and Princess of Wales.

Centenaries of various sorts are to be found, four typical examples being the invention of the Braille system for the

*A plastic marker issued by the Bristol & West Building Society to commemorate the wedding of the Prince of Wales in 1981 (with its presentation slip in the centre) and a colourful paper marker for Queen Victoria's Diamond Jubilee issued by Peter Robinson.*

*Two woven commemorative markers dating from 1977, both issued in informative protective folders. The marker for the Queen's Silver Jubilee was made by J. & J. Cash of Coventry; that for the centenary of St John Ambulance is unattributed.*

blind (1829-1929), the Dorsetshire Labourers (1834-1934), the first public library in Oxford (1854-1954) and the St John Ambulance Brigade (1877-1977). Other commemorative markers can be found celebrating local events such as the opening of a new museum or library.

Commemorative markers are, by their very nature, special issues and they are often more expensively produced. While paper remains the most common material, woven examples are not uncommon, especially for major events, and others are of embossed leather or plastic.

# OTHER MATERIALS

Although most bookmarkers are made of paper or card, other materials are regularly found, notably leather, plastic, wood and various metals. Of these perhaps the most common are of leather.

Early leather markers tend to be a simple flat strip, usually undecorated, but in recent times a distinctive style has evolved. These consist of a flat strip, sometimes fringed at the base, either tooled or printed with a design, often in gold. They are commonly sold in souvenir shops, typically in stately houses, museums, cathedrals and similar popular tourist resorts. The range of both colours and designs is enormous, with examples covering counties, cities, towns, cathedrals and churches, general tourist areas, museums and art galleries, and stately

*Four typical modern leather markers made as tourist souvenirs. These show Exeter Cathedral, Westerham in Kent, a design of birds and a brass of St Thomas à Becket at Cowfold in West Sussex. They are all printed in gold except that the birds are highlighted with four other colours on the white ground.*

homes. The designs are commonly gilt but other colours are found, one complex example featuring a swallow, woodpecker and blue tit printed in four colours on a white ground. One Australian example is cut in the shape of a leaf from one of the country's native trees.

Other materials are less common. Some advertising markers made of celluloid or similar plastic were produced in the early twentieth century. Wooden markers tend to be more recent, often oriental in origin,

*Markers in leather, bone or ivory, plastic and wood. The top one and the two below it are designed to clip over the edge of the page; the plastic marker would date from about 1900 and advertises Robinson's Patent Groats; and the modern wooden marker is probably of Japanese origin.*

sometimes designed as souvenirs. Some are handmade in Australia and decorated with traditional Aboriginal designs. The use of silk declined at the end of the nineteenth century along with the woven markers but it was revived towards the end of the First World War with designs printed on the material rather than woven. Such markers often include a verse, and some were issued as an alternative to 'In Memoriam' cards, normally printed in silver on card edged with black. Markers made of silver, brass, copper or various plated metals are not uncommon, but they tend to take the form of a combined marker and paper-knife.

*Three paper-knife bookmarkers: (left) a thin sliver of pierced wood, probably oriental; (right) plated metal with an enamelled badge of Skegness; and (bottom) Mauchline ware, with a view 'Bridge from South Lowestoft'. In the centre is a silver marker with a long black ribbon, inscribed in 1901.*

## PAPER-KNIFE BOOKMARKERS

The practice of binding books with the papers uncut was common in late Victorian and Edwardian times. The reader had to slit the paper with a knife before the book could be read, and a knife that could be carried in the pocket was preferable. Many bookmarkers were made which could also be used for this purpose. Some were made of stiff card but other materials were much more suitable, including tortoiseshell, celluloid, wood, silver and other metals. The sycamore markers made in Scotland, known generically as Mauchline ware, carry transfer-printed views of towns, cities, seaside resorts or other tourist attractions and were sold as souvenirs. The Scottish family of Smith listed some five hundred scenes in their travellers' albums entitled *Views for Sycamore Work*.

Silver bookmarkers, made for wealthier readers, generally span the period from

28

1880 to 1920, though one example made as late as 1952 has been noted. They consist of a flat dagger-like piece of metal cut to provide a flap which could be slid over the appropriate page. Others have a shorter piece of metal welded to the handle end to serve a similar purpose. Such pieces were hallmarked in Birmingham, Chester and London, and probably elsewhere. Sometimes the handles were decorated with agate, coral, coloured glass or mother-of-pearl. One example has been noted with a solid ivory handle.

Less expensive metal markers were made for sale as souvenirs at seaside or other tourist resorts. These often have enamel coats of arms as decoration on the handle, and the paper-knife type of design survived for these even into recent times, long after the fashion for uncut pages died out.

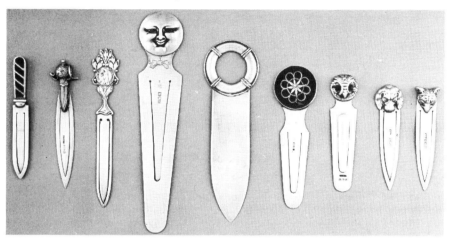

*A collection of papper-knife bookmarkers in silver or white metal. These were hallmarked at Birmingham, London or Chester between 1887 and 1922 and include handles decorated with agate, coloured glass and tortoiseshell.*

*Four paper markers from Europe and America: two from Holland advertising an insurance company and a bookshop; one from France promoting the state railways; and one from the United States with an advertisement on the reverse for 'The Claw – A Story of South Africa' by Cynthia Stockley.*

# BOOKMARKERS FROM OTHER COUNTRIES

Any search for bookmarkers will almost certainly reveal examples from countries other than Britain. These come from all over the world, mainly in books brought in by immigrants or travellers.

Virtually all of the categories described in previous chapters are found from other countries. Some of the most interesting are the advertising markers, such as one from Air France depicting a flying boat with the legend 'Fastest to Four Continents' and another French example showing a streamlined express from the state railways. Some countries issue particularly distinctive markers, good examples being leather markers from South Africa, Israeli markers made with 'genuine handpicked flowers of the Holy Land', wooden markers with Aboriginal designs from Australia, and some particularly attractive pierced bookmarkers from China.

It can be seen that the range of bookmarkers, in terms of subject matter, material, style and purpose, from Britain and elsewhere is vast, and they are full of interest. But let us end this book with words from a bookmarker issued by the Ballarat Public Library in Australia. It is titled:

*A Book's Injunctions*

Don't touch me with dirty hands.
Don't read me if you are unfortunately suffering from an infectious disease (you have my sympathy but please leave ME alone).
Don't expose me to rain or snow
Don't roast me over a fire, your comfort is my destruction. Besides it is unhealthy to stoop and read over a fire.
Don't turn down my leaves at the corners, use a marker instead.

Don't read me at mealtimes.
Don't wet your finger to turn over my leaves because I may get soiled.
Don't use me to keep the window open, heighten the piano stool, nor as a flower pot stand.

Don't abuse me in any way. I am HUMAN because I represent a large portion of my author's mind.
Be very gentle and exceedingly kind to me, so that I may maintain my good appearance and live a long life.

*Four distinctive novelty bookmarkers from around the world: a wooden marker with an Aboriginal design from Australia; a typical leather marker from South Africa; a tourist marker from Jerusalem containing 'hand-picked flowers of the Holy Land'; and a typical pierced paper marker from China.*

# PLACES TO VISIT

Many museums feature a few bookmarkers amongst more general exhibits, particularly if they are of local interest. The only large collection known to the authors may be seen at:
*The Herbert Art Gallery and Museum*, Jordan Well, Coventry, West Midlands CV1 5QP. Telephone: 01203 832381 or 832386.

# FURTHER READING

Baker, J. *Mauchline Ware*. Shire, Princes Risborough, 1985; reprinted 1991.
Browning, D. C. *Dictionary of Literary Biography*. Dent, London, undated.
Coysh, A. W. *Collecting Bookmarkers*. David & Charles, Newton Abbot, 1974.
Curtis, T. *Price Guide to Printed Collectables*. Lyle Publications, Galashiels, 1984.
Evans, Sally. *Bookmarks: An Independent View*. Published for the 43rd Edinburgh Fringe Festival by Old Grindles Bookshop, Edinburgh, undated.
Godden, G. A. *Stevengraphs and Other Victorian Silk Pictures*. Barrie & Jenkins, London, 1971.
Jonker, Abraham. *The Bookmarkers of the Scottish Widows Fund*. Neopardy Publications, Torquay, 1981.
Lewis, John. *Collecting Printed Ephemera*. Antique Collectors' Club, Woodbridge, 1992.
Pinto, E. H. and E. R. *Tunbridge and Scottish Souvenir Woodware*. Bell & Son, London, 1970.
Quayle, E. *The Collector's Book of Books*. Studio Vista, London, 1971.
Rickards, Maurice. *Collecting Printed Ephemera*. Phaidon-Christie's, Oxford, 1988.

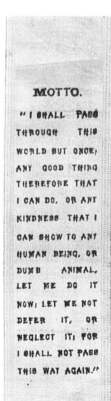

*A very simple old marker made of a length of mauve silk printed with a self-improvement motto.*

*Novelty advertising marker printed in colours and issued by a New York perfumer. This was originally steeped in perfume, of which faint traces still survive.*